FRANCIS FRITH'S

FARNBOROUGH, FLEET AND ALDERSHOT

PHOTOGRAPHIC MEMORIES

STEPHEN PHILLIPS has lived and worked in Aldershot since 1983, where he is Senior Librarian of Aldershot Library. His interests include local, family and military history, and he has been instrumental in setting up the 12,000-volume Military Collection at Aldershot Library. He is also a founder member of the Rotary Club of Blackwater Valley, which he served as President in 1997-8.

FRANCIS FRITH'S
PHOTOGRAPHIC MEMORIES

FARNBOROUGH, FLEET AND ALDERSHOT

PHOTOGRAPHIC MEMORIES

STEPHEN PHILLIPS

First published in the United Kingdom in 2004 by
Frith Book Company Ltd

Limited Hardback Subscribers Edition Published in 2004
ISBN 1-85937-924-9

Paperback Edition 2004
ISBN 1-85937-845-5

British Library Cataloguing in Publication Data

Francis Frith's Farnborough, Fleet and Aldershot - Photographic Memories
Stephen Phillips

Frith Book Company Ltd
Frith's Barn, Teffont,
Salisbury, Wiltshire SP3 5QP
Tel: +44 (0) 1722 716 376
Email: info@francisfrith.co.uk
www.francisfrith.co.uk

Printed and bound in Great Britain

Front Cover: **FARNBOROUGH**, *Lynchford Road c1955* F9020t
Frontispiece: **ALDERSHOT**, *Victoria Road 1918* 68369

*The colour-tinting is for illustrative purposes only, and is not intended
to be historically accurate*

AS WITH ANY HISTORICAL DATABASE THE FRITH ARCHIVE IS
CONSTANTLY BEING CORRECTED AND IMPROVED AND THE
PUBLISHERS WOULD WELCOME INFORMATION ON OMISSIONS
OR INACCURACIES

CONTENTS

FRANCIS FRITH
VICTORIAN PIONEER

FRANCIS FRITH, founder of the world-famous photographic archive, was a complex and multi-talented man. A devout Quaker and a highly successful Victorian businessman, he was philosophical by nature and pioneering in outlook.

By 1855 he had already established a wholesale grocery business in Liverpool, and sold it for the astonishing sum of £200,000, which is the equivalent today of over £15,000,000. Now a very rich man, he was able to indulge his passion for travel. As a child he had pored over travel books written by early explorers, and his fancy and imagination had been stirred by family holidays to the sublime mountain regions of Wales and Scotland. 'What lands of spirit-stirring and enriching scenes and places!' he had written. He was to return to these scenes of grandeur in later years to 'recapture the thousands of vivid and tender memories', but with a different purpose. Now in his thirties, and captivated by the new science of photography, Frith set out on a series of pioneering journeys up the Nile and to the Near East that occupied him from 1856 until 1860.

INTRIGUE AND EXPLORATION

These far-flung journeys were packed with intrigue and adventure. In his life story, written when he was sixty-three, Frith tells of being held captive by bandits, and of fighting 'an awful midnight battle to the very point of surrender with a deadly pack of hungry, wild dogs'. Wearing flowing Arab costume, Frith arrived at Akaba by camel sixty years before Lawrence of Arabia, where he encountered 'desert princes and rival sheikhs, blazing with jewel-hilted swords'.

He was the first photographer to venture beyond the sixth cataract of the Nile. Africa was still the mysterious 'Dark Continent', and Stanley and Livingstone's historic meeting was a decade into the future. The conditions for picture taking confound belief. He laboured for hours in his wicker dark-room in the sweltering heat of the desert, while the volatile chemicals fizzed dangerously in their trays. Back in London he exhibited his photographs and was 'rapturously cheered' by members of the Royal Society. His reputation as a photographer was made overnight.

VENTURE OF A LIFE-TIME

Characteristically, Frith quickly spotted the opportunity to create a new business as a specialist publisher of photographs. He lived in an era of immense and sometimes violent change.

For the poor in the early part of Victoria's reign work was exhausting and the hours long, and people had precious little free time to enjoy themselves. Most had no transport other than a cart or gig at their disposal, and rarely travelled far beyond the boundaries of their own town or village. However, by the 1870s the railways had threaded their way across the country, and Bank Holidays and half-day Saturdays had been made obligatory by Act of Parliament. All of a sudden the working man and his family were able to enjoy days out and see a little more of the world.

With typical business acumen, Francis Frith foresaw that these new tourists would enjoy having souvenirs to commemorate their days out. In 1860 he married Mary Ann Rosling and set out on a new career: his aim was to photograph every city, town and village in Britain. For the next thirty years he travelled the country by train and by pony and trap, producing fine photographs of seaside resorts and beauty spots that were keenly bought by millions of Victorians. These prints were painstakingly pasted into family albums and pored over during the dark nights of winter, rekindling precious memories of summer excursions.

THE RISE OF FRITH & CO

Frith's studio was soon supplying retail shops all over the country. To meet the demand he

gathered about him a small team of photographers, and published the work of independent artist-photographers of the calibre of Roger Fenton and Francis Bedford. In order to gain some understanding of the scale of Frith's business one only has to look at the catalogue issued by Frith & Co in 1886: it runs to some 670 pages, listing not only many thousands of views of the British Isles but also many photographs of most European countries, and China, Japan, the USA and Canada - note the sample page shown on page 9 from the hand-written Frith & Co ledgers recording the pictures. By 1890 Frith had created the greatest specialist photographic publishing company in the world, with over 2,000 sales outlets - more than the combined number that Boots and WH Smith have today! The picture on the next page shows the Frith & Co display board at Ingleton in the Yorkshire Dales (left of window). Beautifully constructed with a mahogany frame and gilt inserts, it could display up to a dozen local scenes.

POSTCARD BONANZA

The ever-popular holiday postcard we know today took many years to develop. In 1870 the Post Office issued the first plain cards, with a pre-printed stamp on one face. In 1894 they allowed other publishers' cards to be sent through the mail with an attached adhesive halfpenny stamp. Demand grew rapidly, and in 1895 a new size of postcard was permitted called the court card, but there was little room for illustration. In 1899, a year after Frith's death, a new card measuring 5.5 x 3.5 inches became the standard format, but it was not until 1902 that the divided back came into being, so that the address and message could be on one face and a full-size illustration on the other. Frith & Co were in the vanguard of postcard development: Frith's sons Eustace and Cyril continued their father's monumental task, expanding the number of views offered to the public and recording more and more places in Britain, as the

coasts and countryside were opened up to mass travel.

Francis Frith had died in 1898 at his villa in Cannes, his great project still growing. The archive he created continued in business for another seventy years. By 1970 it contained over a third of a million pictures showing 7,000 British towns and villages.

FRANCIS FRITH'S LEGACY

Frith's legacy to us today is of immense significance and value, for the magnificent archive of evocative photographs he created provides a unique record of change in the cities, towns and villages throughout Britain over a century and more. Frith and his fellow studio photographers revisited locations many times down the years to update their views, compiling for us an enthralling and colourful pageant of British life and character.

We are fortunate that Frith was dedicated to recording the minutiae of everyday life. For it is this sheer wealth of visual data, the painstaking chronicle of changes in dress, transport, street layouts, buildings, housing, engineering and landscape that captivates us so much today. His remarkable images offer us a powerful link with the past and with the lives of our ancestors.

THE VALUE OF THE ARCHIVE TODAY

Computers have now made it possible for Frith's many thousands of images to be accessed almost instantly. Frith's images are increasingly used as visual resources, by social historians, by researchers into genealogy and ancestry, by architects and town planners, and by teachers involved in local history projects.

In addition, the archive offers every one of us an opportunity to examine the places where we and our families have lived and worked down the years. Highly successful in Frith's own era, the archive is now, a century and more on, entering a new phase of popularity. Historians consider the Francis Frith Collection to be of prime national importance. It is the only archive of its kind remaining in private ownership. Francis Frith's archive is now housed in an historic timber barn in the beautiful village of Teffont in Wiltshire. Its founder would not recognize the archive office as it is today. In place of the many thousands of dusty boxes containing glass plate negatives and an all-pervading odour of photographic chemicals, there are now ranks of computer screens. He would be amazed to watch his images travelling round the world at unimaginable speeds through internet lines.

The archive's future is both bright and exciting. Francis Frith, with his unshakeable belief in making photographs available to the greatest number of people, would undoubtedly approve of what is being done today with his lifetime's work. His photographs depicting our shared past are now bringing pleasure and enlightenment to millions around the world a century and more after his death.

FARNBOROUGH, FLEET AND ALDERSHOT
AN INTRODUCTION

IN MANY respects, the towns of Aldershot, Fleet and Farnborough present something of a conundrum. On one hand they form three distinct entities, which the inhabitants of each town are only too willing to defend; yet on the other hand, they have an inextricably linked history which closely binds them all together.

It is tempting to think that the arrival of the Army in Aldershot in 1854 provided the starting point from which all subsequent events inevitably developed, yet this is clearly not the case. All three towns existed in one form or another long before the first soldier set foot in this corner of north-east Hampshire.

The presence of prehistoric tumuli in the area provides evidence of human activity dating back to long before the Norman Conquest. From the medieval era, too, come several indications of communities that at least survived, even if they didn't always flourish. It has been suggested, for example, that Fleet Pond is of Roman origin; at any rate, it provided the fish for the monks of St Swithun's at Winchester, while the parish church of St Peter at Farnborough has Norman or earlier origins, testifying to a history of nearly

1,000 years. As for Aldershot, it too, has a medieval church, a sprinkling of ancient cottages and a manor house dating from the 17th century.

Yet little hard evidence survives from before the 19th century, when the growth of the rail network in the 1830s and 1840s to Farnborough, and later to Fleet, made hitherto remote areas much more accessible. Although north-east Hampshire lies less than 40 miles from the centre of London, the poor state of the roads meant that a journey to such parts was an undertaking not to be regarded lightly.

The real catalyst was the coming of the Army in 1854, which was to change all this forever. The population of Aldershot at the 1851 Census was a mere 875, while Farnborough's was 477, and Fleet's was too small to be separately counted. Ten years after the Army's arrival and Aldershot's population had increased dramatically to 16,720 while Farnborough's had increased more modestly to 1,600. By 1871 Aldershot's population had increased to 21,682, Farnborough's to 5,744 (although nearly all - 4,260 - were military personnel and their families), and Fleet's numbered only 381. Even in 1891 when

Aldershot's combined civilian and military population totalled 25,595, Farnborough's was only 8,071 of whom more than 5,000 were military personnel and their families in Aldershot North Camp. The same Census showed Fleet's population had risen to 1,171.

So although the arrival of the Army produced the greatest effect on Aldershot, there was also a lesser, but nevertheless similar, effect on Farnborough. Both pre-1854 villages had been loosely centred around their parish churches, but now found their nuclei had shifted somewhat in order to take advantage of the new circumstances. In the case of Aldershot, everything moved a mile or so down the road to be nearer to the Camp, more correctly called South Camp, while in Farnborough a similar move took place from the areas around the church and Farnborough Street in the direction of North Camp, a name which gradually came to describe the whole area around Lynchford Road.

The development of the commercial centres of both Aldershot and Farnborough was to follow a similar pattern, with speculative building springing up in a number of different locations wherever builders thought a quick profit was to be made. As with both High Street in Aldershot, and Lynchford Road in North Camp, these streets were predominantly one-sided, with shops conveniently placed on the opposite side of the road facing the military barracks, ready to maximise their profits.

The development of Fleet was slower in taking effect. The building of the railway station in 1847 meant that the attractions of Fleet Pond were now much more readily available to day-trippers coming down from London; indeed the station was known as Fleet Pond Station until 1869. It was not until 1878, however, that the development of Fleet really began in earnest when Mr Henry Brake of Farnborough paid £4,750 for nearly 250 acres of heathland, which stretched from the Oatsheaf to Avondale Road, to Pondtail and Reading Road bridges. Roads were quickly laid out in the American grid fashion, and plots of land were sold off on easy terms, which in turn led to an increase in the local population. Where large, or increasing numbers of people live,

ALDERSHOT, *Victoria Road 1891* 28667

commercial enterprises follow not far behind, and the opening of Oakley's store in 1885, followed by its later expansion and an accompanying influx of other businesses provide a fine example of this in Fleet.

By the start of the 20th century the population of Aldershot - 30,974 - was not far short of current levels. Aldershot acquired Urban District Council status in 1894, and Farnborough followed suit two years later in 1896. This had the effect of defining the boundaries of local government areas much more tightly than had hitherto been the case, and areas which had until now been considered part of Aldershot suddenly found themselves regarded as part of Farnborough. Nevertheless, in 1901 the population of Farnborough was still only 11,499, of whom 5,098 were military personnel and their families in Aldershot North Camp. Aldershot now found itself hemmed in to the east and south by the county boundary with Surrey, and to the north by Farnborough. Room for growth was suddenly at a premium, while in contrast Farnborough, and particularly Fleet, both had large areas of land in which to expand.

The removal of the Army Balloon Factory from Aldershot to Farnborough in 1905 is a good example of the problems of space faced in Aldershot. Aldershot's loss was certainly Farnborough's gain as the Army Balloon Factory has developed (and undergone several name changes) to such an extent in the past century, that many notable events have taken place there. 'Colonel' Samuel Franklin Cody made the first powered flight in Great Britain in 1908, and less than ten years later, on 1 April 1918, the Royal Air Force was born in Farnborough, the product of the union between the Royal Flying Corps and the Royal Naval Air Service. More recently, in the 1960s, work on the design of Concorde took place at the Royal Aircraft Establishment, as it was then known, and plans for the development of the site will ensure that its links with aviation will not be broken in the foreseeable future.

Aldershot emerged from the years of the First World War confident in its ability to manage its own affairs and consequently set about attaining Municipal Borough status. This was duly achieved in 1922 and for the next 52 years the Borough Council carried out their civic duties with a high degree of efficiency and benefit to the local community, until local government reorganisation brought about a marriage with Farnborough Urban District Council, which produced Rushmoor Borough Council. The provision of the Aldershot Lido and Pools complex was one of the first examples of Aldershot Borough Council's achievements, which later came to fruition when the venue hosted the swimming events of the 1948 Olympic Games. The building of the Public Library in 1954 as part of the many events celebrating the centenary of the Army's arrival in Aldershot was another achievement worthy of mention.

For Farnborough, the growth of the town has continued apace, and in 1961 its population overtook that of Aldershot for the first time. The construction of a brand new shopping centre in Kingsmead and Queensmead in the 1950s and 1960s was undoubtedly a major step forward, providing the opportunity for many new retailers, many of whom were part of national chains, to move into the town. The disadvantage of this has been seen in a corresponding downturn in the fortunes of the North Camp shopping area. But

Farnborough, too, has seen many improvements in recent years. The location of the new Rushmoor Borough Council offices in Farnborough is another example of a suitable site being available there rather than in Aldershot, and other facilities have followed in its wake.

Although Fleet perhaps lagged behind Aldershot and Farnborough in the early stages of its development, it has certainly made up for this in the 20th century. Now not much smaller than Aldershot or Farnborough, it has grown into a busy, bustling town in its own right. The early impetus for the growth of Fleet Road as the main shopping area of the town, was undoubtedly provided by what was to become Oakley's department store, and the opening of branches of businesses from other local towns such as Darracott's bakery and tea rooms from Aldershot, simply cemented this development more firmly in place. More recent additions to the shopping facilities such as the opening of the Hart Centre off Fleet Road have added to the facilities available in the town. A little further along the road, the combined facilities of the Public Library and the Harlington Centre provide fine resources for the

people of Fleet. The recent development of what, in effect, amounts to a new town at Elvetham Heath emphasised the prosperity of the area when it was recently reported to be the second wealthiest postcode area in the entire country.

The recent celebrations in Aldershot of the 150th anniversary of the arrival of the Army provide a convenient moment to pause and reflect on the immense changes that this corner of north-east Hampshire has witnessed. The area has changed from being sparsely populated, sustaining an essentially rural way of life, isolated in nature, to being home to a busy, crowded society, with rapid road and rail connections to London and beyond.

The challenge of the next 150 years will be to build on the changes of the past 150, and to overcome any difficulties in the same way that the problems of the past have been overcome. To put it into perspective, if the rate of population increase of the past 150 years is carried forward into the next 150, the combined population of Aldershot, Fleet and Farnborough would number somewhere in the region of 10 million people by the year 2154! That would be a challenge!

FLEET, *Elvetham Road 1904* 51234

ALDERSHOT

ALDERSHOT
Wellington Street 1892 31112

The premises of Allen and Lloyd, 'Chemists to the Garrison' are on the left, although they were also well-known for producing their own brand of ginger beer and other soft drinks. The Royal Hotel, originally built in the 1850s under the name of Tilbury's Hotel, stands on the opposite corner; it was demolished in 1932. In the distance can be seen the premises of the Capital and Counties Bank which had yet to acquire its second distinctive gable.

◀**ALDERSHOT**
Union Street c1955
A31020

Taken from the opposite
end of the street
approximately 20 years
after 86777 (above), Union
Street still presents a
bustling atmosphere. Two
public houses, the Royal
Arms and the Princess
Hotel are visible as well as
two shoe shops, a jewellers
and a butcher's shop.

Union Street
1935 86777

One of the main shopping streets of the town, this photograph of Union Street conveys something of the bustling nature of the area. Alongside national names such as Timothy Whites, Burton the tailors and Woolworth's, could be found more local enterprises such as White's Tea Lounge a little further up the hill on the right.

◄ALDERSHOT
Union Street
c1960 A31128

A view taken from the junction with Grosvenor Road which shows some of the firms in business in the early 1960s. On view here are the Grosvenor Hotel, Multibroadcast, the Provincial Building Society, Manfield shoe shop, Dunn and Co, Alkit Naval, Military, RAF and Sporting Outfitters, Bata Shoes and Courts Furnishers.

ALDERSHOT
Victoria Road 1891 28667

The Presbyterian church, whose towers
are visible in the distance, was
completed in 1869, although the
building bears the date of 1863.
Evidence of the first stages of
commercialisation can be seen in the
hoarding on the right which advertises
'Show Rooms'. The large building on the
left is the Aldershot Institute, which had
opened three years earlier in 1888.

19

▼ ALDERSHOT
Victoria Road 1918 68369

A generation has passed, and the scene presents an altogether busier view. The gardens of the houses on both sides of the road have been utilised for shop frontages which include two printing works and two photographic studios. The firm of Hunts survived until 1997 and its premises are now occupied by a bedroom furniture shop.

▶ ALDERSHOT
Victoria Road 1927
79623

The junction with Gordon Road and Wellington Street could almost be called 'Bank Corner', as three of the four corners are occupied by banks. The National Provincial building on the right was a relative newcomer, having been built in the early 1920s, while further down, the prestigious Victoria Hotel survived until 1966 when it was demolished to be replaced by shops and offices.

◀ALDERSHOT
Victoria Road
1927 79622

The car in the photograph 79623 (page 20) has now been parked on the left, while its owner has perhaps popped in to one of the two hairdressers, or has maybe crossed the road to buy some flowers from Bide and Sons, or to make a purchase from Godfrey and Co, purveyors of musical instruments.

▶ ALDERSHOT
Victoria Road
c1960 A31158

Another generation has passed since 79622 (above), and the scene has changed to one where the motor car now dominates, forcing pedestrians onto the pavements. Sparks Electrical retailers can be seen on the left, while also visible is Whitby's camera shop on the right, just a few doors up from the Wimpy café which opened in the early 1960s.

▼ **ALDERSHOT,** *Victoria Road c1960* A31159

A similar view to that in A31158 (page 21), although taken a little nearer the junction with Grosvenor Road. The Methodist church, built in 1874, dominates the scene, as it still does today, although in 1991 the building was converted into office accommodation.

► **ALDERSHOT**
*The Heroes'
Shrine, Manor
Park c1965* A31112

The memorial to those who lost their lives in the Second World War includes the statue of Christ stilling the storm which was sculpted by Josephina de Vasconcellos. In the foreground can be seen some of the masonry taken from 56 British cities bombed during the Blitz, and which also forms part of the memorial.

◄ALDERSHOT
High Street
c1955 A31014

The approach to Aldershot from the east runs through the heart of the old village of Aldershot which centred on the area around the Manor House and St Michael's Church. The cyclist in the foreground is passing one of the gates into Manor Park, while ahead can be seen the railway bridge. The railway came to Aldershot in 1870 which greatly aided the development of both camp and town.

► ALDERSHOT
The Football
Ground c1960
A31121

The telephone exchange towers over the 'Rec', home of Aldershot Football Club. Football League members for 60 years until 1992, they were reborn as Aldershot Town and began the long climb through the non-league pyramid until in May 2004 they narrowly failed in an agonising penalty shoot-out to regain their league position.

ALDERSHOT
Cargate Avenue 1898
42014

Taking its name from 'Cartgate', this area is mentioned in the 'Crondall Customary' of 1568, but it was not until the 1870s that the area began to be built upon. It quickly became one of the more sought-after areas of Aldershot, providing homes for many of the town's leading citizens

ALDERSHOT
The Swimming Pool c1955
A31010

The development of Aldershot Park Estate in the 1920s was one of the first major projects of the newly-chartered Aldershot Borough Council. The old lake was drained and converted into a bathing pool, although the original contours were retained. The pool was often described as the finest in the south of England, a claim which received a measure of support when the Municipal Bathing Pool became the venue for the swimming events at the 1948 Olympic Games. The outdoor pool continues to be a hugely popular attraction during the summer months - weather permitting!

▶ **ALDERSHOT**
High Street 1931
83730

A largely deserted view, possibly taken on early closing day, which would have meant this was a Wednesday afternoon. The Empire Cinema is showing 'The Queen's Husband', starring Lowell Sherman and Mary Astor, one of the very early talkie films to be made. Across the road in the building with the semi-circular gable end are the premises of William May and Co who for many years published Sheldrake's 'Aldershot Military Gazette', which in 1859 was Aldershot's first local newspaper.

◀**ALDERSHOT**
High Street 1938 88360

A few changes have taken place in the seven years since the photograph 83730 (above) was taken. The most notable is the building of the Ritz Cinema next to the Empire, and the street certainly is a lot busier than in the earlier view. The shops on the right testify to the wide range of services available at the time: Stephens and Johnson, ironmongers; Bateman, forage contractor; Flights Military Outfitters; the Magpie, sweets and cigarettes; Orange, chemist and optician; and Salter's sports shop. Note, too, the shops' different architectural styles, although they all date from the last quarter of the 19th century.

▲ **ALDERSHOT,** *High Street c1955* A31022

Seventeen years have passed but very little has changed on this stretch of High Street. Perhaps the people on the left are strolling down to the café in the Empire Cinema before seeing a film either there or in the Ritz next door.

◀**ALDERSHOT**
Princes Gardens
c1955 A31043

As can be seen from this photograph, this was a popular spot to sit and relax on a sunny summer's day. The Princes Gardens had been the site of the first temporary military encampment in November 1853 when a detachment of Royal Engineers began assessing the locality's suitability for the establishment of a permanent military base.

THE MILITARY

ALDERSHOT
The Naafi Club c1960 A31083

Opened in 1948 by the Duke of Gloucester, the Naafi club dominated the junction of High Street, Wellington Avenue, Gun Hill and Station Road until its demolition in 1985. On the right, a pub bearing the name of the Royal Exchange has stood on this site since at least 1855, although it has now been converted into residential accommodation.

ALDERSHOT
The Cambridge Military Hospital c1960 A31098

The first large-scale military hospital to be built, it is named after the Duke of Cambridge who performed the opening ceremony in 1879. The hospital cost £45,000 to build, provided 260 beds and has a corridor running through the building, measuring 176 yards in length.

ALDERSHOT, *All Saints' Church 1891* 28671A

Diverging from High Street at the junction with Station Road, Wellington Avenue led directly to the 'Cathedral Church of the British Army'. Built in 1863 by the well-known architect of the time, P C Hardwick, it still maintains an imposing presence at the top of the town, despite the more indirect route to it now followed by Wellington Avenue.

ALDERSHOT
*Wellington Avenue
1891* 28669B

Once a hugely popular and colourful spectacle in Aldershot, the Sunday morning church parades used to attract large crowds. The large number of Army bands in the town at any one time generally meant there was no lack of opportunity for music lovers!

ALDERSHOT, *Wellington Monument 1891* 28673

This imposing statue of the Duke of Wellington seated on his horse, Copenhagen, has been situated on Round Hill since 1885, when it was brought from Hyde Park Corner in London where it had dwarfed the Constitution Arch since 1846. Recently cleared of obscuring undergrowth, it has now been restored to something like its former glory.

▲ ALDERSHOT

The Clubhouse 1892

31114

Like many early military buildings in Aldershot, the driving force behind the Officers' Clubhouse was Prince Albert, the Prince Consort. The Clubhouse was built in 1859 and had changed very little when this photograph was taken. The site is now occupied by Potter's International hotel.

▶ *detail from 31114*

34

ALDERSHOT
'C' Lines 1892 31119

The first, tented, military encampment of 1854 soon gave way to row upon row of 'temporary' wooden huts which, however, survived well into the 1890s. They were arranged in 'Lines', designated A to Z, each one providing accommodation for a battalion, or equivalent. They finally gave way to brick-built huts which, in turn, have now largely been demolished, to be replaced by a variety of modern buildings.

ALDERSHOT, *Talavera Barracks 1918* 68373

One of the earliest permanent buildings in military Aldershot, dating from the 1850s, these buildings served as home to countless soldiers for a century, before being swept away in the frenzy of post-war rebuilding.

◄ **ALDERSHOT**
Queen's Avenue
c1955 A31055

The arrow-straight course of Queen's Avenue can be seen here looking north towards its eventual junction with Lynchford Road in North Camp. The church spire is that of St George's Garrison Church, the foundation stone of which was laid by Queen Victoria in 1892.

◄ **ALDERSHOT**
Infantry
Barracks 1891
28675

The barracks blocks were connected by a huge glass roof, the purpose of which was to enable the troops to engage in drill during wet weather. This was removed in the early 1900s after a number of fatal accidents had occurred to soldiers engaged in cleaning the roof.

◄ **ALDERSHOT**
Queen's Avenue and
Queen's Parade 1928
80784

Apart from the lack of traffic, remarkably little has changed since this photograph was taken. The large grassy area behind the trees on the right is Queen's Parade through which runs the Aldershot-Farnborough boundary. The area is so-called after the many reviews of troops held there under the gaze of Queen Victoria.

▲ ALDERSHOT
North Camp Gymnasium and the Swimming Baths 1905 53264

The gymnasium was opened in 1894 to reflect the growing emphasis the Army was placing on physical fitness. The swimming pool followed three years later, thus removing the need for would-be swimmers to use the altogether less suitable and hygienic Basingstoke Canal!

► *detail from 53264*

ALDERSHOT
The Command Fire Station 1896 37154

With the large number of wooden huts built in the military camp, the provision of a fire station was essential. One of its more notable actions came in 1902 when it was called to a fire in the Queen's Hotel, North Camp. Unfortunately, its efforts were to no avail and the hotel was destroyed. The building to the left with the clock tower is the Marlborough Lines Infants' School, formerly the Garrison School.

ALDERSHOT, *North Camp, Brigade School 1905* 53282

The school's tower can be seen in the background of photograph 37154 (above), and was one of the first schools to be built specifically for the children of military personnel. The school is still in use today as the Marlborough Lines Infants' School.

► **ALDERSHOT**
North Camp
Connaught Hospital
1903 49325

Built in 1897, the hospital
was named after the Duke of
Connaught, General Officer
Commanding at Aldershot
from 1893 to 1898. Sadly, the
building was demolished in
1989.

◄ **ALDERSHOT**
Connaught Hospital 1905
53266

The Connaught Hospital, together with the Cambridge Military Hospital, received the first intake of wounded soldiers of the First World War at the end of August 1914. For many local people, this was the first news from the front since the outbreak of war nearly four weeks earlier.

CIVILIAN NORTH CAMP

FARNBOROUGH
Lynchford Road 1905 53259

Similar to High Street in Aldershot, Lynchford Road is largely one-sided, having grown up to serve the troops who were largely based on the left-hand side of the road in this photograph. One of the placards outside C H Senior's shop refers to a report in the 'Aldershot News' of the Army Cup Final; for the record, 2nd Battalion Grenadier Guards beat the Service Battalion, Royal Engineers by 2-1.

FARNBOROUGH
Lynchford Road
c1955 F9022

The one-sided nature of the road is clearly visible in this photograph, taken approximately 50 years after 53259 (pages 42-43). The premises of Clem Yates & Co were also just visible in the distance of the earlier picture, and provide a link with the days when the army still relied heavily on horses for its transportation.

FARNBOROUGH, *Lynchford Road c1960* F9090

Five years on from F9022 (above) and Clem Yates' sign advertising forage has disappeared from the wall of the building which the lorry is just passing. As the then main shopping area of Farnborough, two shoe shops are in evidence, and just beyond the North Camp Hotel is Hewett's butchers' shop.

FARNBOROUGH
Lynchford Road
c1960 F9087

A view looking in the opposite direction from that in F9090 (page 44), showing Timothy Whites, and beyond that, Boots the Chemist. The lack of people in both pictures suggests this may have been taken on a Wednesday, which was early closing day.

FARNBOROUGH, *Lynchford Road c1965* F9179

Another five years have passed since F9087 (above) was taken, and the main difference is in the appearance of the North Camp Hotel. The ornate balustrade has been dismantled leaving an altogether less imposing façade to look down the length of Queen's Avenue.

FARNBOROUGH
Camp Road c1965
F9176

Looking towards the
junction with Lynchford
Road, a rather downmarket-
looking Fine Fare
supermarket with what
appears to be a corrugated
iron roof has managed to
gain a toe-hold, next to the
more substantial Linney's
electrical appliance shop.
Note, too, the pair of
spectacles hanging from the
shop on the right; these
were the premises of
Morton's opticians.

▲ FARNBOROUGH
Camp Road c1965
F9177

Looking north from Lynchford Road this time, it can be seen that Timothy Whites have crept round the back of Boots the Chemist and have established a presence on both Camp Road and Lynchford Road itself.

▶ *detail from F9177*

FARNBOROUGH
Camp Road c1965
F9233

Taken from a little nearer the junction with Queen's Road than F9177 (page 48), the wide range of shops in North Camp can clearly be seen. A bingo hall has taken over the Scala cinema, and if your numbers have come up, you can spend your money across the road in Pet's Quest pet shop or P A Baker's television store, or if your win has been really spectacular, you can always buy a 'good used car' from Keetella's Garages a little further down the street.

FARNBOROUGH, *Peabody Road c1965* F9232

Providing a mixture of both residential and commercial property, Peabody Road was still enough part of the shopping centre to be able to boast Curzon and Son's betting shop, Tottles' newsagents, the Robinsons family grocer's shop with the Wavy Line sign, and across the road, on the corner with High Street, B & R fruiterers.

▲ FARNBOROUGH
Peabody Road c1965
F9183

Looking in the opposite direction to that in F9232 (page 49), towards Lynchford Road, some of the shops from that previous photograph can be seen from a slightly different angle. Wally's fish and chip shop and the Bran Tub toy shop on the left give further evidence of the mixed nature of the street.

▶ *detail from F9183*

▲ **FARNBOROUGH**
Alexandra Road
1919 68916

Originally developed during the 1880s to provide housing for army officers, Alexandra Road also contained some commercial buildings as the London County and Westminster Bank - now the NatWest - testifies. The omnibus advertising Park and Sparkhall, drapers of Aldershot, is bound for Aldershot Railway Station.

◀ *detail from 68916*

FARNBOROUGH AND COVE

FARNBOROUGH
Town Hall c1965 F9228

Situated on Alexandra Road at the junction with Reading and Guildford Roads is the Town Hall. Built to the designs of architect George Sherrin in 1897, the building reflected the growing stature of the town, and now enjoys listed building status, although now in use as office accommodation under the name of Ferneberga House.

▶ **FARNBOROUGH**
*Queensmead
Shopping Centre
c1965* F9153

◄ **FARNBOROUGH**
*Queensmead Parade
c1965* F9208

Hitherto, Farnborough's
commercial centre had been
firmly based in North Camp,
but with the decline in the
numbers of military
personnel the decision was
taken to build a brand new
shopping centre more easily
accessible to residents of
both North and South
Farnborough. Fine Fare
supermarket's premises on
the right of F9153 (above)
compare favourably with
those shown in North Camp
in F9176 (page 46), while
many of the other typical
High Street retailers seem to
have become quickly
established in the new
shopping centre.

▲ FARNBOROUGH
The Royal Aircraft Establishment 1913 65203a

Evolving from the Army Balloon Factory, which moved from Aldershot to Farnborough in 1905, into the Royal Aircraft Factory in 1911, before becoming the Royal Aircraft Establishment in 1918, this was the scene of Samuel Franklin Cody's first powered flight in Great Britain in 1908. Sadly, Cody was to die in an aircraft accident in 1913, the year this photograph was taken.

▶ *detail from 65203a*

▲ **FARNBOROUGH**
The Swan Hotel
1913 65197

Clearly recognisable today, the Swan was opened in 1861 by a Mr George Swann and the name of the pub may well have been a pun on his surname. Note the many bicycles propped up outside, while in the distance a horse-drawn cart can be seen approaching.

◀ *detail from 65197*

57

▼ **FARNBOROUGH**
Tumbledown Dick 1936 87234

An inn has stood on this site for over 300 years, although the origins of its name are in dispute. The most plausible theory is that it was named after Richard Cromwell, son of Oliver, who bore this somewhat scathing nickname. Legend also has it that Dick Turpin once slept here, and as a result, lent his name to the inn.

▶ **FARNBOROUGH**
The Clockhouse 1936 87232

Built in 1895, this landmark has changed only a little since this photograph was taken, the main difference being the removal of the columns which had become too weak to bear the weight of the cupola. The somewhat leafy scene has changed hugely, however, a busy roundabout now occupying the road junction.

◄ **FARNBOROUGH**
*The Old Parish
Church 1897* 39029

Easily the oldest
building in
Farnborough, the
parish church of
St Peter dates from
about 1200, although
there is evidence to
suggest a Saxon
church may have
occupied the site
before then. Inside the
church there are wall
paintings of three
female saints dating
from when the church
was first built.

► **FARNBOROUGH**
*The Parish Church
c1955* F9048

The 17th century
weatherboarded tower
is an unusual feature,
and is believed to have
been constructed from
ship's timbers. The
lychgate was
constructed in 1907 in
memory of Major and
Mrs Holt of
Farnborough Grange.

◄**FARNBOROUGH**
*Homestead Farm
1906* 55638

Dating from the 17th
century, Home Farm's
outbuildings to the
right of the picture
have been
demolished and
made way for Home
Farm Close, while the
farmhouse itself on
the left still stands.
Note the soldier in
uniform on his horse,
passing the entrance
to the farmyard.

◄ FARNBOROUGH
Farnborough Street, Ye Olde Farm 1903 49323

This 17th century building was owned for many years by William Smith, potter and farmer, until his death in 1858. Smith's life is recorded by his grandson George Bourne in a book published in 1920. The farmhouse has now been converted into four separate cottages.

◄ FARNBOROUGH
Victoria Road c1955 F9044

Williamson the grocer occupies the foreground on the right, while the row of shops beyond with the awnings down are the premises of Wright Brothers, general drapers. In the far distance can be seen the inn sign of the Alexandra public house.

FARNBOROUGH, *Victoria Road 1913* 65184ax

Situated in one of the main shopping streets of North Farnborough, this row of three shops include the Victoria Fish Supper Bar and D B Davies bicycle shop, while nearest the camera is a ladies and gentleman's outfitters shop.

▲ FARNBOROUGH
The Alma 1913
65189

No less than three pubs can be seen in this photograph of Cove Road. The Alma is in the foreground on the right, while the three upper windows of the Anchor can be seen a little further along. On the opposite side of the road the Tradesman's Arms claim that 'cyclists are provided for' is backed up by the three bikes leaning against the wall of the pub!

◀ *detail from 65189*

63

▼ **COVE,** *The Village c1955* C172008

A view similar to 65189 (page 63), but taken approximately 50 yards further along and 50 years later. Little appears to have changed, even to the extent of the lack of traffic in the later photograph, which must have been unusual, even in 1955! The Anchor has since undergone a change of name to the Old Court House, in recognition of a tradition that it once was the venue for court proceedings.

► **COVE**
Prospect Road 1913
65190

Looking towards Prospect Road across the present-day site of Cove Green Pavilion, Cove Pond gradually disappeared with the introduction of improved drainage systems, with the result that the Pond was totally drained by the early 1950s. Much of the area is still open land, however, in use as allotments.

◄ COVE
West Heath Corner 1913
65194

The premises occupied by Brown's sweet shop on the left, and W Wright, draper, outfitter and boots and shoes are now used as offices and a Chinese takeaway restaurant, and the whole scene is now transformed by a large roundabout on the right-hand part of the photograph.

► COVE
Fleet Road 1913
65195

Evidence of the westward development of Farnborough can be found in this picture, showing houses along Fleet Road. These houses were built in the very first years of the 20th century, with a great deal of the development taking place between 1902 and 1906.

FLEET
TOWN
CENTRE

FLEET
Market Place 1907 57430

Following the building of Oakley's department store in the 1890s, the cupola of which can be seen on the right, this area of Fleet Road was known as the Market Place. The name never really caught on, however, and by about 1920 had fallen into disuse.

▶ **FLEET**
Fleet Road 1903 49220x

Oakley's department store has become a well-established business, with its cupola providing a focal point for the whole shopping area of the town. There is a display of boater hats in the window, and perhaps the gentleman driving his horse and trap just outside purchased his top hat there, too?

▼ *detail of 49220x*

FLEET, *Market Place 1903* 50768

The unmade nature of the road is clearly visible in this photograph. The large shop on the right is Darracott's tea rooms and bakery, while a display of gentlemen's clothing can be seen hanging outside the next door shop.

FLEET, *Oakley's Stores, Market Place 1906* 53707x

The impressive façade of Oakley's Stores simply oozes prosperity as it faces the larger department store premises across Fleet Road. The smaller shop nearer the camera is A E Bond who sold toys, stationery and fancy goods. Note the two large gas lamps hanging from their shop front.

◄ **FLEET**
Fleet Road 1924 75264

Still a mixture of residential and commercial properties, Fleet Road is nonetheless well on the way to becoming Fleet's principle shopping street. The awning of Laslett's shop is just visible on the extreme left, while private houses are vying for room with neighbouring shops.

◄ **FLEET**
*Market Place
1920* 69908

The roads have now been tarmacced, and more shops have opened up. Oakley's is still going strong, as is Darracott's opposite. Next door is Pratt's fruit stores while a little further along, a sign proclaiming 'This is Laslett's' advertises the Fleet branch of the outfitters and drapers, originally founded in Aldershot.

◄ **FLEET**
Fleet Road 1924 75262

Ernest Oakley had taken over the running of the family business from his father James in 1918, but it was very much 'business as usual' for, amongst other things, the store is advertising furniture for sale and bottled ales and stout from its off licence.

FLEET
The Post Office
1907 57435

FLEET, *Fleet Road 1907* 57436

The Post Office had occupied these purpose-built premises for only one year when this photograph was taken, having previously occupied G E Page's milliners and draper's business three doors along. Between the two are the hairdresser's shop of E Phillips and the tailor's shop of William Hewison.

FLEET
Fleet Road Bank
1907 57432

The Capital and Counties Bank on the right of the photograph bears the date of 1834 which, however, refers to the founding of the bank rather than the date of the building which occurred in 1898. The premises are still devoted to banking today, and are clearly recognisable in photograph F32029 (page 74) as the home of Lloyds Bank.

FLEET, *Fleet Road 1920* 69907

Motorised transport is in the process of taking over from more traditional methods, while the three small boys on the left have to make do with two bikes between them! The Capital and Counties Bank is still very much to the fore, while the premises of Mellor's jewellers shop are somewhat overshadowed next door.

▼ **FLEET**
Fleet Road 1924 75265

The Capital and Counties Bank is plainly visible in the middle distance on the left, with Barclays Bank more clearly seen on the right. An omnibus is trundling along the street in the far distance, and note also the roadworks in front of the chemist's shop.

▶ **FLEET**
Fleet Road c1965 F32029

Not yet choked by traffic, the parked vehicles nonetheless provide a clue as to the shape of things to come. Westminster and Lloyds banks on the left and Boots the Chemist in the distance on the right bear witness to the commercial nature of the road.

◄ **FLEET**
Fleet Road
c1965 F32028

Taken from very close to the same spot as F32029 (page 74), but facing in the opposite direction, this picture gives further evidence of the development of Fleet Road as the commercial centre of Fleet.

► **FLEET**

The Oatsheaf Hotel
1903 50770

Built in the 1840s and therefore one of the oldest buildings in Fleet, the hotel is externally little changed today. Situated at the southern end of Fleet Road, it profited greatly from the expansion of Fleet in the last years of the 19th century, and when this photograph was taken offered 'good accommodation for commercial gentlemen, parties, cyclists, etc.' The sign on the wall above the horse and cart proclaims the hotel's name and advertises 'Everard's Extra' to potential customers.

OUT AND
ABOUT IN
FLEET

FLEET
The Wesleyan Church 1903 49226

Built on the corner of Fleet Road and Branksomewood
Road in 1899 to replace a smaller, wooden church
dating from 1887, the church continued in use until
1966, three years after uniting with the Reading Road
Methodist Church. The building was sold the following
year, demolished, and the site is now occupied by
Woolworth's.

FLEET
*All Saints' Church
1903* 49222A

The Squire of Crondall, Mr Charles Lefroy laid the foundation stone of All Saints' in August 1860 in memory of his late wife. Unfortunately, Mr Lefroy himself died the following April, leaving the work to be completed by Mrs Lefroy's father, Sir James Walker at a cost of £3,323. The church was finally consecrated in 1862.

FLEET, *The Lake 1903* 49714

Of man-made origins, possibly in Roman times, the Lake, or Pond, was certainly in existence as a source of wild fowl in Saxon times. Always a haven for wildlife, in 1951 it became a Site of Special Scientific Interest, owing to its importance for both fauna and flora.

▲ **FLEET**
Clarence Road 1908
60072

One of the early
developments in
Victorian Fleet, Clarence
Road links Reading Road
South and Kings Road.
This photograph was
evidently taken in high
summer, as the child in
the pram is well sheltered
by her parasol.

◀ *detail from 60072*

**CHURCH
CROOKHAM**
*Aldershot Road
c1960* C102013

Built-up by the early
years of the 20th
century, this was one
of the roads
developed in order
to cater for Fleet's
expanding
population. Shops,
filling stations and
churches punctuated
the housing from the
beginning, as they
do today.

CHURCH CROOKHAM, *Christ Church c1960* C102010

The church was built in 1840-1 to serve the needs of a growing population at a time when the nearest church was three
miles away in Crondall. It cost £3,351 to build, over a quarter of which was raised by local people, the remainder being
supplied by the local gentry.

▲ CROOKHAM
The Street 1910 63036

The Black Horse is instantly recognisable today, despite the passage of nearly 100 years. The local children have come out in force for the benefit of the photographer, while in the far distance can be seen the Post Office and store run by William Jassett.

◀ *detail from 63036*

81

◄**CHURCH CROOKHAM**
Sandy Lane 1910 63035

The top-hatted gentleman on his cart is thought to be Mr May, known as 'Cabby', who was presumably seeking customers for his horse and trap. The scene today has been transformed by the construction of a roundabout to ease traffic flow.

◄ **CROOKHAM**
The Street 1910
63037

The road has not been tarmacced; the lack of traffic meant that it was not high on any list of priorities! The young lady standing in the road has no cares about being run over, while the group of boys on the grass by the signpost appear to be simply admiring the view! The signpost points left to Dogmersfield, Winchfield and Odiham, while the right hand points to Crondall and Farnham. Straight on lies Fleet and Church Crookham!

◄ **CHURCH CROOKHAM**
The Village 1903
49233

The Wyvern Arms, now simply the Wyvern, was built by the Lefroy family of Crondall in the 1860s. The winged mythical creature was their emblem, and inn-building was something of a departure for them as hitherto they had supported and built several churches in the neighbourhood.

▼ **CHURCH CROOKHAM**
The Wyvern c1960 C102017

The pub has changed little since the earlier photograph 49233 (page 83), although the road has, of course, been tarmacced in the interim. Although still very wooded in appearance, the area has nonetheless become slightly more urban, as evidenced by the cars and the houses on the extreme left.

► **FLEET**
The Basingstoke Canal 1908 60080

Started in 1788, the canal linked Basingstoke to the River Wey near Godalming, but struggled to make a profit throughout its existence. The flat towpath was clearly an attraction for cyclists nearly a century ago, as it continues to be today.

◄ **CHURCH CROOKHAM**
Malthouse Bridge 1906 53712

The name of the bridge reflects the local trade which once existed in the area and, as in 60080 (page 84), the level nature of the towpath was an attraction for walkers 100 years ago, as it was for cyclists. This part of the canal is also popular with anglers.

► **FLEET**
Reading Road 1903 49716

The house on the right is the Beacon, one of the more substantial residences in Victorian and Edwardian Fleet. Properties such as this gave rise to the description of 'The Blue Triangle', reflecting political affiliations of the day, and the term is still much in vogue among estate agents today.

FLEET
Elvetham Road 1904
51234

The lack of other vehicles meant that it probably didn't matter too much, but the driver of the horse and trap is apparently unaware of the 'keep left' rule of the road. However, the number of wheel marks on the road surface would indicate that even in 1904 this was a well-used thoroughfare.

87

FLEET
Minley Road 1903 50772

The rural nature of this scene is emphasised by the cart just visible inside the barn, and the boy with his barrow about to cross the road. A building can just be seen through the trees in the centre of the photograph.

INDEX

NAMES OF SUBSCRIBERS

The following people have kindly supported this book by subscribing to copies before publication.

John Berio, Farnborough

Doris & Ronald Boyd

Mrs L Brown, Aldershot

Mr M J Burke, Mrs B J Cole, Fleet

The Callow Family, Cove, Farnborough

Mr D R & Mrs M J Christopher

The Cottington & Millis Family

Peter Cullen

The Curtis Family, Farnborough

Andrew Denning Davies, Aldershot

Barry Denning Davies, Farnborough

Heather Maureen Davies, Farnborough

In memory of A G S Dawes, Farnborough

Mark Deacon, Farnborough

Norman Eastment, Farnborough

Miss K Farthing

P W Gallow

The Gardner Family, Farnborough

Mrs M Gough, Fleet

Mr T Griffiths & Mrs P Griffiths

J Hearn

Mr T A & Mrs C J Hinton, Fleet

Joan & Mike Hughes, Cove

The Hunneyball Family, Ash Vale

C R & J A Hunt, Farnborough

Dave & Ros Jordan and family, Nik & Cara

C Kempson, Farnborough

Gladys & Bert Kennedy, Aldershot 2004

G Lewis

John W Lofts, Farnborough

Nicholas E Milbourn, Farnborough

The Mint Family, Farnborough 2004

Carol A Norbron, Farnborough

W G Oldfield

John Parker

Roger Price

John L Pullen, Fleet

In memory of my parents, S & G Quickfall

The Rawlings Family, Farnborough

Roger & Mary Read, Farnborough

William & Pauline Shaw, Aldershot

Richard & Maria Smith Family, Farnborough

K W Stewart

The Strudwick Family, Ash Vale

Mr P H Taylor

Mr & Mrs A Turnbull, Cove

Ward Family, Ash Vale

John R & Eleanor J Webb, Fleet

The Wiggins Family

The Worstencroft Family

FRITH PRODUCTS & SERVICES

Francis Frith would doubtless be pleased to know that the pioneering publishing venture he started in 1860 still continues today. Over a hundred and forty years later, The Francis Frith Collection continues in the same innovative tradition and is now one of the foremost publishers of vintage photographs in the world. Some of the current activities include:

Interior Decoration

Today Frith's photographs can be seen framed and as giant wall murals in thousands of pubs, restaurants, hotels, banks, retail stores and other public buildings throughout the country. In every case they enhance the unique local atmosphere of the places they depict and provide reminders of gentler days in an increasingly busy and frenetic world.

Product Promotions

Frith products are used by many major companies to promote the sales of their own products or to reinforce their own history and heritage. Frith promotions have been used by Hovis bread, Courage beers, Scots Porage Oats, Colman's mustard, Cadbury's foods, Mellow Birds coffee, Dunhill pipe tobacco, Guinness, and Bulmer's Cider.

Genealogy and Family History

As the interest in family history and roots grows world-wide, more and more people are turning to Frith's photographs of Great Britain for images of the towns, villages and streets where their ancestors lived; and, of course, photographs of the churches and chapels where their ancestors were christened, married and buried are an essential part of every genealogy tree and family album.

Frith Products

All Frith photographs are available Framed or just as Mounted Prints and Posters (size 23 x 16 inches). These may be ordered from the address below. From time to time other products - Address Books, Calendars, Table Mats, etc - are available.

The Internet

Already fifty thousand Frith photographs can be viewed and purchased on the internet through the Frith websites and a myriad of partner sites.

For more detailed information on Frith companies and products, look at these sites:

www.francisfrith.co.uk
www.francisfrith.com
(for North American visitors)

See the complete list of Frith Books at:

www.francisfrith.co.uk

This web site is regularly updated with the latest list of publications from the Frith Book Company. If you wish to buy books relating to another part of the country that your local bookshop does not stock, you may purchase on-line.

For further information, trade, or author enquiries please contact us at the address below:
The Francis Frith Collection, Frith's Barn, Teffont, Salisbury, Wiltshire, England SP3 5QP.
Tel: +44 (0)1722 716 376 Fax: +44 (0)1722 716 881   Email: sales@francisfrith.co.uk

See Frith books on the internet at www.francisfrith.co.uk

FREE PRINT OF YOUR CHOICE

Mounted Print
Overall size 14 x 11 inches (355 x 280mm)

Choose any Frith photograph in this book.
Simply complete the Voucher opposite and return it with your remittance for £2.25 (to cover postage and handling) and we will print the photograph of your choice in SEPIA (size 11 x 8 inches) and supply it in a cream mount with a burgundy rule line (overall size 14 x 11 inches).
Please note: photographs with a reference number starting with a "Z" are not Frith photographs and cannot be supplied under this offer.
Offer valid for delivery to one UK address only.

PLUS: Order additional Mounted Prints at HALF PRICE - £7.49 each (normally £14.99)
If you would like to order more Frith prints from this book, possibly as gifts for friends and family, you can buy them at half price (with no additional postage and handling costs).

PLUS: Have your Mounted Prints framed
For an extra £14.95 per print you can have your mounted print(s) framed in an elegant polished wood and gilt moulding, overall size 16 x 13 inches (no additional postage and handling required).

IMPORTANT!

These special prices are only available if you use this form to order . You must use the ORIGINAL VOUCHER on this page (no copies permitted). We can only despatch to one UK address. This offer cannot be combined with any other offer.

Send completed Voucher form to:
The Francis Frith Collection, Frith's Barn, Teffont, Salisbury, Wiltshire SP3 5QP

CHOOSE A PHOTOGRAPH FROM THIS BOOK

Voucher for **FREE** and Reduced Price Frith Prints

Please do not photocopy this voucher. Only the original is valid, so please fill it in, cut it out and return it to us with your order.

Picture ref no	Page no	Qty	Mounted @ £7.49	Framed + £14.95	Total Cost £
		1	Free of charge*	£	£
			£7.49	£	£
			£7.49	£	£
			£7.49	£	£
			£7.49	£	£
			£7.49	£	£

Please allow 28 days for delivery.
Offer available to one UK address only

* Post & handling		£2.25
Total Order Cost		£

Title of this book . . . .
I enclose a cheque/postal order for £ . . . .
made payable to 'The Francis Frith Collection'

OR please debit my Mastercard / Visa / Maestro / Amex card, details below

Card Number

Issue No (Maestro only)   Valid from (Maestro)

Expires   Signature

Name Mr/Mrs/Ms . . . .
Address . . . .
. . . .
. . . .
. . . . Postcode . . . .
Daytime Tel No . . . .
Email . . . .

Valid to 31/12/07

Free Print – see overleaf

Would you like to find out more about Francis Frith?

We have recently recruited some entertaining speakers who are happy to visit local groups, clubs and societies to give an illustrated talk documenting Frith's travels and photographs. If you are a member of such a group and are interested in hosting a presentation, we would love to hear from you.

Our speakers bring with them a small selection of our local town and county books, together with sample prints. They are happy to take orders. A small proportion of the order value is donated to the group who have hosted the presentation. The talks are therefore an excellent way of fundraising for small groups and societies.

Can you help us with information about any of the Frith photographs in this book?

We are gradually compiling an historical record for each of the photographs in the Frith archive. It is always fascinating to find out the names of the people shown in the pictures, as well as insights into the shops, buildings and other features depicted.

If you recognize anyone in the photographs in this book, or if you have information not already included in the author's caption, do let us know. We would love to hear from you, and will try to publish it in future books or articles.

Our production team

Frith books are produced by a small dedicated team at offices in the converted Grade II listed 18th-century barn at Teffont near Salisbury, illustrated above. Most have worked with the Frith Collection for many years. All have in common one quality: they have a passion for the Frith Collection. The team is constantly expanding, but currently includes:

Paul Baron, Phillip Brennan, Jason Buck, John Buck, Ruth Butler, Heather Crisp, David Davies, Louis du Mont, Isobel Hall, Gareth Harris, Lucy Hart, Julian Hight, Peter Horne, James Kinnear, Karen Kinnear, Tina Leary, Stuart Login, David Marsh, Lesley-Ann Millard, Sue Molloy, Glenda Morgan, Wayne Morgan, Sarah Roberts, Kate Rotondetto, Dean Scource, Eliza Sackett, Terence Sackett, Sandra Sampson, Adrian Sanders, Sandra Sanger, Jan Scrivens, Julia Skinner, David Smith, Miles Smith, Lewis Taylor, Shelley Tolcher, Lorraine Tuck, Amanita Wainwright and Ricky Williams.